The Begatting of Ronald Reagan

The Begatting of Ronald Reagan

Lincoln Haynes, Michael Malone and Myron Roberts

•

Drawings by John Beshears

PALOS VERDES BOOK COMPANY
LOMITA, CALIFORNIA

ISBN 0-936848-03-0

Palos Verdes Book Company, P.O. Box 456,
Lomita, California 90717.

Manufactured in the United States of America

THE UNAUTHORIZED VERSION

From the Scribes
to the Pharisees

Chapter and Verse

Chapter I

up!

I

Jericho, D.C.

NOW IT CAME TO PASS THAT FOR 40 years the liberals ate the fat and drank the sweet, for they had the Keynes to the Kingdom. And the conservatives wandered in the wilderness of the Sun Belt, for there was no room at the Holy Day Inn.

Then they came upon a freeway that turneth unto the right, and upon it was writ this sign:

"Myrrh, Frankincense and Lodging. Next Turnoff."

Whence the conservatives followed hard upon the supply side until they came to the wicked city of Jericho, D.C.

Now Jericho was straitly shut up and girded round with thick walls of bureaucracy, so that no new ideas went out and none came in. And within, the Democrats laughed and danced, for the New Deal had become an old shuffle with a stacked deck.

But it came to pass that the Republicans multiplied, yea, even unto a Moral Majority. For where there had been Commandments in the number of 10, they made Propositions like unto 13.

Chiefest among them was Ronald, a Gentile Joshua, and they named him Rawhide that he might smite the Democrats' ass.

And Ronald summoned unto him seven preachers with seven rams' horns and told them to blow hard that the walls might Falwell. And they blew their tubes, and the walls came tumbling down.

Then Ronald spake on this wise: "Shout, for the Lord GOP hath given ye the city, and all the silver and gold shall come unto the Treasury. Let us lay out a safety net for the truly greedy."

Now the Republicans were in the countinghouse,

and the land flowed with mink and money. And Ronald was anointed king, and he decreed that the rich should pay no tax, toll or tribute, and he held out the promise of salvation, tax-free, for All Soul-Savers.

But there came a stripling who took up a sling against him and slang it, and Ronald was sore afflicted, though he jested at his wounds.

Whereupon Alexander the Ingrate went forth before the people, saying: "Yea, verily, thus do I scenario ye. Unto ye I caveat the status quo, for a Haig in command is worth two of the Bush, and I am No. 1."

Still whilst Ronald lay wounded he dreamt a dream on this wise. He saw a great White Tent, and therein were those of high degree, men of renown, and they feasted upon plates of gold and deeds of trust.

Then Ronald was made whole. And when he returned he said unto the people, "Give a hungry man a fish, and he will hunger yet again tomorrow; but teach him to fish, and he shall ne'er hunger again."

Wherefore he subtracted the loaves and fishes from the budget and decreed no loaves for loafers. But the Democrats called it a fish story; neither would they let him turn ketchup into vegetables.

Then Ronald sliced the welfare rolls thin, and when the poor cried out, he threw them a Laffer curve, for this was the pitch according to the Law of the Profits.

And the people sat in darkness and cried out, "Let

there be light." Yet Reagan gat but one Watt, who turned wine into polluted water and oceans into oil wells.

And Ronald sent forth Caspar the Wine Burgher unto all nations and warned them to put no SALT in Brezhnev's borsht. And they builded hard silos and filled them with all manner of A-Bombinations. And Ronald gave the world a B-1 complex and made the Saudis AWACS-fat.

Then Khadafy, who had been Billy's angel, became Ronnie's devil. And Ronald strove to make his polls rise as the Poles fell. And when the nations cried "Peace, peace," he threw them a red herring.

For now the summer was past, and the shadow of war and recession fell across the land. And the people were sore and afraid.

Chapter II

PETERS '81

II

Bored Again: The Book of Jimmy

IN THE BEGINNING GOD CREATED a place called Plains, in the backside of Georgia. And the South was void, and darkness was upon the heart of the segregationists.

And the Lord God planted a garden therein, and

he said, "Let this earth bring forth peanuts abundantly." And lo! there were peanuts, and they were good for crackers.

And the Lord God said, "Let us make a goodly ol' boy after our likeness. And let him one day have dominion over the biggest fish in the sea, and the foulness of the air, and all creepy things upon the Earth."

And God said, "Let a child be born unto a Lily of the Plains." And He created Jimmy. And God saw that this was good enough.

Now when Jimmy was but a youth, he saw that the daughters of Plains were fancy, and he knew lust in his heart. Wherefore he went into the wilderness for 40 days and prayed, lest he be counted among the fornicators of this world, the drinkers of strong drink and the swearers of oaths.

Then the Lord God took pity on Jimmy and brought him a young virgin full of grace and truth, and her name was called Rosalynn, a damsel of the new ERA. And they went faithfully unto the House of the Lord together and had good checkups, wherefore was Jimmy saved from his sinful imaginings. And he acquired the ruling passion.

Then it came to pass that an angel of the Lord appeared and said: "Thou art the man. Go thou, Jimmy, and lead thy people unto a land of peanut butter and jelly."

But Jimmy was sore afraid, saying: "I am slow of

speech, wherefore will not the media mock me? For many are called, but few are chosen."

But the angel said unto him, "Fear not, Jim boy. The race is not to the swift, nor the battle to the strong. Eat thy grits, and grit thy teeth. Get thee unto the people, and tell them the South shall rise again, for this day a new King is born. And to those whose necks are red as the Georgia clay, speak of faith, hope and parity."

So it came to pass that Jimmy went to and fro across the land, and walked up and down in it crying, "My name is J.C., and I'm running for Savior."

But he was as a voice crying in the wilderness, for the media knew him not and asked: "Jimmy who? What manner of man is this?"

And the party chieftains laughed and said: "Peanut vendor, what monkey business is this? Go climb a poll."

Whereupon J.C. answered them: "Great men are not always wise. Yet am I come to lead the people out of sin." And he reproached those who sat in the wicked city of Washington, saying: "Thy secretaries type not, but make Hays while the sun shines. And the Mills of the Congress grind Fannys, not corn."

Then came to him Hubert, a mighty champion of the Democrats. And he said unto Jimmy: "What is this Dixieland jazz? Thine ancestors were planters and slave masters, yet the black folks, still they cotton unto thee."

And J.C. answered him thusly, "Except that a man be born again, he shall not win the nomination."

Then J.C. prophesied in this wise: "Verily, I say unto thee, he that dwelleth on the Hill is flesh, but he that riseth from the Plains is of the spirit. Wherefore if thou or Kennedy runneth, yet shall I whip yo' ass."

And Hubert was not baptized, for he feared to jump in.

Then there rose the young chieftain Jerry, from the California Kookdom, who would be King before his time. But though he could cross wits like a Jesuit and cross legs like a Buddhist, and though his temples were snowy, still they called him flaky. And they cast him back into the Sacramento River, wrapped in swaddling clothes.

Then J.C. went unto a place called Iowa, and Jimmy cracked corn, but they didn't care. And he went to Florida and smote Wallace in the primaries. And thus was he chosen among all Democrats.

Now did J.C. sally forth to battle Ford the Pharaoh. But lo! this Ford was not a Lincoln, and a slow starter. For when he fled the Nixon camp he looked back and forgave Richard his trespasses, wherefore was he turned into a pillar of the party.

And the people gave him the Watergate, and Jimmy was chosen. And so it came to pass that a square sat in the Oval Office.

Now J.C. summoned his disciples unto Washington. And he threw down the pastry chefs, and he exalted men of low degree, saying, "Let them eat crackers," and they wandered through the White House a-pickin' and a-grinnin'.

Jimmy lifted up his Lance, a mighty money-changer, who multiplied peanut loans beyond redemption until the media called it a shell game. And the Lance was broken.

Then came Schlesinger, the messenger of bad tithings, who was overlord of energy until he runneth out of gas.

And Andrew the Younger, who heeded not the elders of the tribe but chewed on the forbidden Arafat. Wherefore was he accused of bad mouthings and banished from the Council of Nations.

And there was Billy, the second son of Lillian, whose station it was to sell provender for the camels; a man who had no better thing under the sun than to eat and drink and be merry. For beer was in the navel of his belly, and he was jes' Plains folks and did give merriment unto the media.

Even a fool when he holdeth his peace and his water is counted wise, but Billy did go on TV and say, "Wouldst drink my beer from my pitcher?" And he delivered himself unto the Libyans and cursed the Israelites. And the people were sore amazed, and when the scribes sought J.C.'s words concerning these abominations, he asked, "Am I my brother's keeper?"

Now there was much talk of faith without works, and the people despaired of their leader. Therefore, J.C. walked upon the mountain at Camp David, and he labored mightily but brought forth a malaise.

Then J.C. delivered his staff into the hands of Ham, son of Jordan. But when the comely damsels of Washington crossed Jordan, he spat Amaretto into their secret places and called it Southern Comfort. And he journeyed into the sinful discos of Gotham and the wicked Hills of Beverly and sniffed out the evil therein.

And the people looked over Jordan, and what did they see? Another good ol' goy.

Chapter III

OIL

III

Ayatollah and the 40 Thieves

NOW IT CAME TO PASS THAT THE land of Iran was ruled by a mighty Pharaoh, who owned an ocean of oil and burned it at both ends. He was called Shah Pahlavi, and he palavered with the Israelites and the elders of Zion, which was not protocol.

And the Shah liked gold exceedingly, wherefore did he shill for Shell. And he took the people from the fields and brought them unto the cities, where they knew television and watched "Dallas" and sundry abominations. And they ate of alien porn. And the Shah sent their sons unto the land of J.C., where they lay down beside the liberated maidens and ran from the Koran.

Wherefore there rose up among them a false prophet whose name was Khomeini, and he was the champion of the Persians against the Kurds and the Nerds. And his hand was against the land of J.C., for he was the Sword of Islam, a chopper off the old block. Wherefore did the Shah banish him, hoping he would croak among the Frogs.

Yet whilst in exile Khomeini builded a flame in the hearts of his people, and the Shah felt the heat. Wherefore did he leave home—but not without his American Express card.

Then Khomeini hustled his tail and flew back on a wing and a prayer, and thrones were cast down. And there was the Devil to pay.

And the Ancient of Days did sit, his head as white as snow, his eyes like burning fire. A fiery stream came forth from his mouth, and ten thousand times ten thousand stood before him. But his judgment was set.

Whereupon Khomeini went before the media and

cursed J.C. and cried, "Verily I am holier than thou." He put a hex on Exxon, and he chastened Chase Manhattan. And the Earth shook and the world trembled. And the Arabs caught gold fever. And the oil companies were aghast, wherefore they raised the price of gas.

Now this Khomeini went unto the people preaching hard-Koran. And he gave them the Persian Version, in this wise:

Lest the young men cleave unto the maidens, he banished the women singers and the men singers, and the Song of Solomon was purged from Tehran's Top Ten. And he lashed the whores and put to death the whoremongers, and bade the fair damsels drape themselves in sackcloth and called the young chicks fowl.

And he cut off their hands, lest the people reach out and touch someone. For he was a holy terrorist.

Then the people were sore amazed, and they turned off their TV and turned on to pistachio nuts and goats. And they went into the streets and raised Khomeini's likeness high and scourged themselves in the backsides for the sins of the Shah. And Khomeini fed them with gall and wormwood.

And he cursed the children of Israel and cut off their oil, that they might freeze their assets. For he was the biggest bigot, lower than the PLO.

Now it came to pass that the Shah was covered

with boils, wherefore he had the gall to seek entry unto the land of J.C. And he went unto David and his Brethren crying, "I ran Iran for ye; now why have ye forsaken me?"

So they bade J.C. take him in, and oiled the gate. And J.C. hearkened unto them, for the election drew nigh, and the voice of the Brethren ringeth loud and clear.

And they had their physicians succor the Shah, but lo! he suckered them.

Now there stood in the land of Persia a great household called the Embassy, and therein dwelt many wise counselors and brave men to guard against the wolves of the night, and comely maidens who laid their hands to their typewriters and clave to the keys, yea, even unto overtime.

Now it came to pass that the proud Persians waxed wroth at the Americans for taking in the Shah, and vice versa. Wherefore they assembled a great host of students who liketh rifles better than books, and they banged upon the Embassy door and cried, "Pray, let us join ye, for ye are the apple of the Ayatollah's eye."

In this wise did they enter therein, and they fell upon the people of the Embassy and bound them. And thus began the days of the Iranian Captivity.

And the Shah took his ease at his watering place, saying, "Ayatollah you so."

Now the Persians rushed into the streets and made great noise, and it was heard far off, yea, unto NBC. And the Ayatollah trimmed his beard, and his eyes glittered like unto Satan's, and he gave his blessing unto those evil deeds and vowed to slay the fatted calves on prime time. But the Americans could CBS.

Wherefore the heart of J.C. was troubled, and he cried, "Behold, our diplomats are betrayed into captivity at the hands of the infidel," and he sweated great drops of oil.

Then J.C. retired unto his Rose Garden and fasted and prayed and wept before the media. And his sleep went from him, and he cried with a lamentable voice that the captives should have no damage — and he should have no blame in the campaign. And he set aside all business of state.

And he sent his messengers unto the captains and the kings of this Earth, that they should lay sanctions upon the Ancient of Days. But the kings answered softly that oil and troubled waters mix not. And the Ancient of Days still held fast to the hostages and said that each would be judged according to the law of the Medes and Persians, which altereth not.

Then J.C. girded his loins and cried out, "Let my people go." And he sent many ships of war into the gulf, and threatened to part the Red Sea. And the Air Force was with him, and he raised high his craven image.

Then a vision came upon the head of J.C., and he saw eight great winds of heaven chopping across the sea. And they were exceedingly strong and had great iron teeth and would devour and break into pieces the Iranians.

So it was that the Great Speckled Birds landed in the desert, and there was darkness and confusion in the swirling sands, and the ignorant army clashed by night. For an ill wind blew it, and the choppers couldn't cut it.

Then a caravan of Bedouins rode up—but the Marines had missed the bus. So the great birds laid an egg, folded their landing gear and stole away in the night. Thus the mission was aborted, and Iran called it an illegal abortion.

Then Vance walked out, for he found it a mission implausible. And Brzezinski smiled in the shadows. And at the White House the No. 1 Square was back to Square 1.

Then J.C. went before the Council of Nations, and together they bade Khomeini, "Open sesame." But the Ayatollah and his 40 thieves hearkened not until it was too late for J.C.

For yea, verily, they had him over a barrel of oil.

Chapter IV

ERA

IV
The Urban Cowherd

NOW THERE AROSE A STAR IN THE West called Ronald, albeit he was of the second magnitude and was known for B-attitudes. And he moved from left to righteous, wherefore the Republicans praised God for one who was saved among the sinners who burnt incense in the hills of Hollywood. For he was a straight-shootin', God-fearin', tax-dodgin' patriot.

And Ronald went unto the swimming pools of the liberals, and the idolators of the fleshpots, and cried out against those who sacrificed their first fruits unto the Golden Cad. And he went before the tube, and he ruled over the Valley of Death.

Now the Democrats were keepers of sheep and lived off the fat of the lambs. And the Republicans were owners of cattle and tillers of the land who landed in the till. Wherefore Ronald put on his white hat and rode out of the Valley of the Shadow of TV and into the wasteland of politics, that he might purge the land of the rustlers of votes. And he spread the light according to GE, saying, "Yea, verily, he that increaseth welfare increaseth sorrow."

And he said, "Cast not thy bread upon the Feds, neither shall ye swim in the Red Tide, lest ye surely drown. Get thee instead unto the banks, for the banks giveth and the banks taketh away."

And his solution found favor with the solvent, so that his spread increased, and men trusted his deeds and honored his trust deeds, and his cattle grazed across a hundred hills.

Wherefore he became Governor of California, and still he paid no tax, toll, tribute or custom. And he was sheltered.

Then it came to pass that the noise of war was heard in a far-off land, and the far-out cried, "Hell, nay, we goeth not." And the young men lay down beside the still maidens.

And when Ronald heard of this abomination, he cried, "Verily, I shall defoliate these flower children." And the sound of the posse was heard in the byways of Berkeley, and they smote them in their sanctuaries, hippie and thigh.

Hence was Ronald's favor noised about among the righteous, the keepers of God's lawns.

Now it came to pass that in the reign of the wicked King Richard, a band of robbers stole into the sanctuaries of the Democrats, that they might hearken to the song O'Brien. But they heard instead the song of the sirens. And they were brought before a proud Roman judge, who said unto them, "Break not, neither shall ye enter," and gave them everlasting life.

And when the scribes did go unto King Richard to inquire who had fathered this immaculate conception, he answered them, according to his cunning: "I know not. Mayhap it was of virgin birth."

Wherefore was he crucified upon the *Washington Post.* And there was a falling off, and he disappeared in a pillar of fire.

So it was that Ronald went into the primaries and strove mightily, but the right wing would not fly, and he was rear-ended by a Ford. And it fell to J.C. to rule the land, wherefore Ronald turned westward to the range to mend his fences. And still the dumb beasts loved him, for on his ranch were many mansions.

Then another election came upon the land, and it was time to ride and rope them in again. So once again Ronald did put on his white hat, his crown of glory, and the hair beneath was black as a raven's right wing, though the days of his years were nigh upon threescore and ten. And men said that he knoweth not the Grecian Formula.

And he cried, "My strength faileth not." But his enemies whispered, "Men do not put old whines into new bottles."

And they sent a Baker against him, but his dough would not rise. And the giant Connally rode forth from the land of milk funds and money, but he soured early and was creamed. And many set out upon the campaign trail, but Ronald dropped them in their tracks.

Wherefore those who could not beat him did join him, and Ronald and his righteous ones rode into Motown, the city of the chariot makers, and stampeded the convention.

For his faithful companion, Ronald looked at the new Ford, but the payments were too high. Then he saw the Bush that burned not, until Ronald lighted a fire under him, and together they went before the assemblage. And there was great jubilation and a laying on of hands and a laying off of the issues.

Whereupon the assemblage bowed before Ronald and washed his feet, lest they stray too far right, praised him and anointed him with moderation. And he praised FDR and promised every woman jewels of silver and gold if she goeth not whoring after the ERA and aborteth not the fruit of the womb. And they prayed for the Old Glory and cursed the New Morality.

And together they went forth to battle the band of Georgia rednecks and Georgetown pinkos, lest the freaks should inherit the Earth. For it was High Noon, and time to move 'em out.

Chapter V

V
The Ted Commandments

OW THESE ARE THE GENERATIONS of the sons of Joseph, of the tribe of Saint Patrick.

This Joseph was a mighty man, and he builded him many mansions at Hyannis in the Land of the Cod, and he had many manservants and maidservants. Yet there was famine in the land, and the Republicans gat no wine. Wherefore Joseph drew wine from the leg of his boot, and the people grew merry, and Joseph grew exceeding rich. And he made a great prophet.

Wherefore he sacrificed unto the Almighty FDR, who was well pleased with his Irish long green and sent him to the court of Saint James. And Joseph dreamed that one day he would be King.

But he wined and dined many concubines and became a patsy for the Nazis. Therefore when FDR saw that Joseph had sinned, he put a curse upon him, even unto all his sons. And Joseph's first-born died on the wings of the Great Speckled Bird as the children of God waged war against the Hitlerites.

Then Joseph called his remaining sons before him and charged them thusly: "It is written that my sons shall be kings; therefore be fruitful and multiply, and scatter my seed even unto the Rose Garden." And the clan ran.

It came to pass that the next-born son, John, found favor in the eyes of the people, for his words were gracious, and he lifted up their spirits and caused men to walk upon the moon. And when the wicked Muscovites sought to put him in a pocket with a rocket, he turned their missiles into millstones. And it came to pass that John rode in his chariot through the wicked city of Dallas, that the rulers therein might anoint him with oil. But the curse of death rode with him.

Then the next-born son, Bobby, sought to reign in his brother's place. But he, too, was slain, even in the City of Angels. And the Angels wept. For it was a time of woe and great affliction, as all Israel lay scattered upon the hills like sheep that have not a shepherd.

Thus it fell upon the last-born son, Teddy, to fulfill the prophecy of Joseph to beget Israel with new life. But an unfunny thing happened on the way to the White House.

It came to pass that Teddy gathered his manservants and maidservants, and they builded a fire upon the Cape of Cod and barbecued the fatted calf. Their hearts grew merry with strong drink, and they were laid back, while in a far place Joan drank alone.

Then a comely damsel came forth with her pitcher on her shoulder and said unto Ted, "Wouldst thou draw water with me?" And the joints of his loins were loosened, and they went beyond the vale in the dark, and lo! their chariot fell from the bridge at Chappaquiddick.

Then Teddy went before the people on TV, and the Holy Ghost writers washed away his sin. But his enemies called it a fish story and swallowed it not. And they charged him:

"Thou hast cast thy broad upon the water, and it shall come back to thee."

Now it came to pass that the South did rise again, and J.C. was made King. And he did spurn the chariot appointed to carry him from the place of his anointing, and he did mute the silver trumpets that would hail him as the chief.

Still the people remembered Camelot and were not well pleased, and they turned to Teddy, youngest son of Joseph, who labored mightily on the Hill. But Teddy went often before J.C. and bowed himself and said: "Yea, verily, I believe. Forgive me mine unbelief." And he wandered in the wilderness unto the fourth year.

Then it came to pass that inflation and recession were visited upon the land, for there was no bread, neither was there gasoline. And the money-changers grew fat whilst the people wept upon their everlasting bills. And they cried out, "Teddy, save us."

And the scribes and publicans came unto him and showed him their polls. And Teddy turned the other cheek, and he mustered his minions and his millions and shouted, "My kingdom cometh."

Wherefore he wandered into the network and slipped in Roger's Mudd. For Teddy was slow of speech.

So he went before the people; up and down the land he walked, and to and fro in it. And as the days passed, his heart lifted and his delegates increased in number. But they were weighed and found wanting.

Thus the Democrats gathered in the city of Gotham, where they were seven days in labor, that they might bring J.C. to term. And he was born again.

But lo! there was a thick cloud, and the delegates were lost therein, and knew not left from right. Then Teddy came down from Mount Hyannis, and he spake to them thusly:

"I bring ye the commandments of FDR, and they are graven on these planks for your platform:

"I am the Lord thy God, which have brought thee out of the House of Hoover.

"Thou shalt not worship groovy images, for they are bad actors.

"Honor thy prime rate, and keep it lowly.

"Honor thy father and thy mother with Social Security.

"Honor thy brother, lest he become a foreign agent.

"Honor thy ERA, lest the hand that rocketh the cradle shall cradle the rock.

"Honor the stranger within thy gates, lest he be the tax collector.

"Honor the New Deal and keep its works, that thy term in office may be multiplied.

"Thou shalt not kill, save only in the Lord's holy wars against the Germans, the Japanese, the Koreans, the Chinese, the Vietnamese, the Cambodians, the Laotians, the Iranians, the Libyans, and above all the godless Russians, which are an abomination before the Lord.

"Thou shalt not kill any welfare program.

"Thou shalt not worship the Golden Calf, nor go whoring after the Rand of Kruger.

"Sacrifice not unto the Pentagon, neither shalt thou build an altar of brass."

And his words were softer than oil, though there was fire in his heart. And the delegates cheered and said, "How forcible are right words." And he held them in his hand, and they were his.

Wherefore did Teddy go with J.C., and he feinted at him with damned praise.

And he bideth his time four more years.

Chapter VI

VI
I Never Promised Ye a Rose Garden

AND IT CAME TO PASS THAT J.C. was home in the Rose Garden, for he was of common clay, albeit half-baked. And he was naked of ideas, but not ashamed.

Then the Lord God came unto him and said: "Of

the fruit of every tree in the garden thou mayest eat. But of the fruit of boredom thou shalt not eat, lest thou drive the people up the garden wall."

And J.C. fell into a deep sleep and he dreamed a dream on this wise:

There appeared unto him seven sisters whose beauty and fame were noised throughout the land, and their names were Exxon, Gulf, Shell, Arco, Chevron, Mobil and Texaco. And men lusted after them, for they were premium under the hoods.

The seven sisters grew rich beyond measure, and they feasted like fat things, until the people cried out:

O, J.C., by the pumps of Exxon we lined up.
We wept, for her breasts were dry.
And we were as children
Whose mothers gat no gas.
Lead us back unto full service,
Yea, even unto free glassware.
Forgive us our credit cards
And check again our dipsticks.
Deliver unto us the keys to the rest rooms
That we may be comforted,
And anoint us with oil.
Remember us now and in the moment of running on empty,
Lest in the Day of the Re-election we forget thee.

Now when J.C. awoke from his dream he was ahungered, and he ate of the fruit from the tree of boredom, for he was an unoriginal sinner. And when God saw this, He grew wroth. And J.C. was ashamed and raised up the prime rate to cover his nakedness.

And God said: "I never promised ye a Rose Garden. Because thou hast done this thing, thou shalt crawl for re-election on thy Billy. The blacks shall eat not of thy Plains white bread, and Ronald shall rise up and close thy pearly gates."

Wherefore J.C. and Rosalynn went across the land seeking votes, saying, "We're doin' the best we kin."

Now Ronald, too, went to and fro across the Earth, giving absolution from pollution. And though he was old, still he appeared strong and lusty, for he was a man of war. And Nancy sought to nip Rosalynn in the bud.

Now there arose another challenger, the white-haired Prophet John, who cried: "We unhappy few are strong as many. Where two or three are gathered in my name, there am I." And he called upon the followers of J.C. to join his caravan.

And sundry others coveted J.C. his mansion. There was Barry the Commoner, but he was not common enough. And the leader of the Libertarians chimed in, but this Clark runneth backward.

Now although Ronald prayed with the Gentiles, yet also he promised the Jews that he would shut the gates of Jerusalem against the infidels. And to the people he cried out:

"J.C. is thy shepherd; ye shall surely want. He leadeth ye beside the still umemployment lines; he maketh ye to lie down beside the Red bastards."

And J.C. heard the people murmuring and he said to Ronald, "I can rant as well as thou ravest." And he whipped up the Cold War with an Afghan fan and an Olympic ban.

"I am the Prince of Peace, descended from Camp David," he cried, yet his warships bristled with missiles, and he dealt with Stealth.

Now John began to fall back, and he cursed his fate, saying, "Comfort me not with rotten apples." But it was in vain, for he went against a stone wall, wherefore he grew sore of head and hard of nose. And men called him a spoiler.

And Ronald did go before certain zealots who were called the Moral Majority, for they thought to lower the wages of sin, and they were sick of love. And he moved closer to Formosa, for they were holier than Mao.

Wherefore the people grew afeared, and his counselors whispered unto Ronald: "Make no friendship with angry men. Let not thy left wing know what thy right wing doeth, and ad-lib not, lest thou be at liberty."

And Ronald sheathed his sword and dined on dove, but without SALT. He changed that which was writ on his 3-by-5 scrolls, and he strove mightily to remember parity with clarity, and that the Common Market was not Safeway. And he promised to raise up a skirt unto a judge's robe.

Still J.C. went to and fro across the land, stirring up apathy, and his days grew few and full of trouble. And he promised manna from Atlanta, but this matzoth was a dry cracker.

Then it came to pass that J.C. challenged Ronald to single combat, and Ronald rose to de bait. And both were washed and anointed that they might go unto the networks to make witness before the people.

And J.C. spake of Amy, and how the little child had led him, but out of the mouth of this babe came a bomb. And Ronald spake of a debt-laden donkey and promised, "Yet shall I lift this burden off thine ass."

Still alone in a far corner stood the Prophet John, flailing at shadows, for yea, verily, three was a crowd.

And the day of the election was at hand. But NBC cried out, "He who casts the first ballot hath decided all." And the followers of the Prophet John pierced J.C. on the left side, and the Israelites brake him with a Billy club on the right. And when the roll was called down yonder, J.C. wasn't there. And there was a landslide, and the mountain fell on J.C. And once more the people jeered, "Jimmy who?"

Whence cometh Ronald yet again on the Late Show, and the people cheered and anointed him. And there was an Exodus of the Liberal Tribe.

Then Ronald said, "For 40 years, and then some, have ye wandered in this wilderness. Rejoice, for I have found my sheep which were lost."

And thus it was that Ronald foreclosed on the Rose Garden. For yea, verily, the money-changers were back in the temple.

THE BEGATTING OF RONALD REAGAN continues a series by the same authors which began with THE BEGATTING OF A PRESIDENT, an irreverent satire on the Johnson and Nixon years in pseudo-Biblical style. A best-selling book and Grammy-nominee comedy record by Orson Welles, it was followed by the 1972 BEGATTING. A combined edition of all three is planned.

About the Scribes

Lincoln Haynes, Michael Malone and Myron Roberts view the political scene with heavily jaundiced eyes from three widely scattered Southern California suburbs, where they work as writers, editors and teachers.

Haynes and Roberts were born in Los Angeles, were co-founders of *L.A.* magazine and have also written for the *Saturday Review, Nation, Los Angeles Times* and many other magazines and newspapers.

Malone, born in England, is a U.S. citizen and long-time resident who has contributed to various magazines and written two college textbooks with Roberts.

About the Artist

John Beshears is from Missouri, where he was born, graduated from the University of Missouri and was an artist on the Columbia *Daily Tribune.* A Vietnam veteran, he is now a staff artist on the Long Beach *Press-Telegram* in California.

Cast Thy Bread
Upon
the Writers